Am...

*We live, we breathe, we laugh,
we love*

*Through courage and strength, we
rise above*

*We conquer, we confess, we risk
it all*

*for that one real chance, to
truly fall*

*Obstacles are encountered,
through every opened door*

*though curiosity, leaves us,
opening more*

Faith compels us, to believe

*anything is possible, it's up to
us to achieve*

*We all have a vision, a dream in
mind*

*Ambition is the outcome, that's
hard to find*

*When the mind is set, nothing
stands in the way*

*to achieving the dreams, we held
one day*

*Bridges are burned, in the dead
of night*

*it's up to us, in choosing, the
path, that's right*

*Through courage and strength, we
choose to win*

*allowing our destiny, to truly
begin*

Breathe

Be still the sounds of a beating heart

broken, bruised and torn apart

Silence the burdens hidden within

we don't come to lose, we come to win

Vanquish the fears hiding inside

its our own rules that we abide by

Throw ourselves into loving arms

its here we're free and release those harms

Silence the madness inside our head

never wish that you were dead

Life is cruel and times are hard

but they always turn over a brand new card

Deal with the cards that you
were dealt

remember the great feelings that
you have already felt

Instead of striving on the bad

think of the great times that
you've already had

More will come you just have to
wait

take a breather and lessen your
plate

If you are at this point you
need a break

and this is one that you should
take

Relax, be happy, make a plan

if you think you can't, believe
me "YOU CAN!!"

You can do it, you will see

and happily ever after you will be

Motivation

We live to fight another day, some
will leave but some will stay

We fight to see that rising sun that
lets us know our search is done

We wish upon a shooting star that
faith is seen and not too far

We dream a dream, our hopes held high
and in that dream fate will fly

Visions and dreams we see for ourselves
can always be accomplished
within yourselves

In order to make your dreams come true
believe in the faith that lives in you

Motivation is keen on having that drive
that can cause just anyone to strive

Strive towards your dreams no matter what
ignoring the urge to add the but..

As long as you belive in yourself, just you,
there is nothing stopping you, from what you can do

Wisdom

If something is scary, take the risk

If your gravy is lumpy, use a whisk

If you fail the first time, try again

If you think you're going to lose, try harder to win

If you think you're wrong, make it right

If you want to give up, don't, just fight

If you're scared to death, face the fear

If your mind is foggy, make it clear

Follow your heart despite the pain

Acting crazy makes us sane

If you've felt the pain of a bleeding heart

Put it back together, part by part

If you're holding a grudge, just let it go

Heal the heart and let it show

Take the risk and feel alive

Start to live, not only survive

TRUST

There was a girl, she had a past

Thrown into a world, where nothing could last

Hurt, betrayal, all the works

Hiding the truth, it comes with perks

Keep to myself, I'm stronger than that

Fake sympathy is all you get, when you decide to chat

Do you want to be looked down at, as weak?

No, you don't, you are strong, don't speak

Keep it inside, hide the hurt

If you get drunk, you're going to blurt

Think again, what is the deal?

No one truly cares, about what you feel

Look at your mom, she let it happen

Who cares that it was you, girl you need a slappin'

OH! Your dad, so mighty is he

He chose that woman, purely over me

Acts like he cares, because he's now alone

But truth be told, his evil was shown

Your family, your friends, who's that again?

You're all alone, think hard as sin

You can help, to an extent

But you can't be helped, your feelings are spent

You're the strong one, can't be weak

Don't even think, to let it leak

There is too much, you're lost in vain

Damned to earth, to feel the pain

You've been molested, beaten and broke

But you always got up, you didn't choke

You saved your sister, isn't that enough?

Forget the rest, just forget that stuff

I can't forget it, it's much too deep

Hiding inside, when I want to leap

Off the edge, down from the roof

Disappear from earth, just gone, spoof!

The pain it hurts, too much to bear

But I can cry, there's no need to share

I am strong, I am built so tough

But, sometimes it feels, it isn't enough

What did I miss? My turn I guess

Just hide the feelings, can't accept any less

These are mine, I hold them dear

I don't want to live, in a life of fear

Got to get up, Got to get going

Look at me, I'll soon be glowing

I can do it, I'll make it through

It's in my blood, my mind is true

There you go, now you're talking

Come on now, get to walking

You can do this, a strong mind

You have a heart, and it's not blind

Find your place upon the land

Don't keep sinking, in deep quicksand

When you feel weak, think of me

I am your mind, and I'll set you free

Free from the pain, free from the hurt

Free from the chain, upon your shirt

I'll weigh you down and test your strength

But my commitment, has no length

I'm here to the end, all along the way

To help you anytime, you are feeling astray

I'll lead you back, won't leave you lost

And the best part is, I come at no cost

Believe in me, and you will be fine

With me you can never, ever cross the line

We are one, one in the same

Now aren't you glad, that I have came?

I do feel better, you have a way

Together we will always stay

My feelings are mine, they hide so kind

Down real deep, where no one can find

The pain I feel is mine to bleed

Someone to trust, it's what I need

If I hide too long, I'll never be found

I'll be lost forever, and don't like the sound

Now, now, child, listen to me

You and I, is how it's got to be

You let them in, they bring you hurt

I won't allow it, you're mine to flirt

I won't hurt you, I'm kind and sweet

I'll fight the pain with you, I'll never cheat

I'll keep you safe, forever and ever

Trust someone else, now that's not clever

It's you and me, against it all

Go out and search and you will fall

Deep in love, just like before

And what did you get? Hurt even more

Please don't do this, you're all alone

With me you don't even, need a phone

Just look inside, that's where I lay

I am you, and I do not play

You listen to me, I have to try

I have to hope, they will not lie

I have to pray, that they are true

Just as me, and just as you

We are one, so you can see

That this is truly, how it must be

If I don't trust, how can I know?

If my life truly is, just a show

Many years, I've felt this way

And all the years that left, the feelings stay

I can't hide this any longer

If I get hurt, it will only make me stronger

But if I try, I did my best

And then who cares, about all the rest

I've been through worse, and came back

So why now, must I slack?

I won't give up, I simply refuse

This is my life, and I will choose

I will do, what I feel is right

And in the end, I've won the fight

Tell me now, what do you say?

Will you help me, along the way?

I trust you, you trust me

So I feel that this must be

We will fight, we will argue

But to ourselves, we're always true

We will make the right choice

We have a stance, we have a voice

If times get tough, we'll turn around

But deep inside, we'll always be found

Let's get started, where to begin?

You, my dear, have a battle to win

This is me

Restless feelings in the mind
happiness, it appears, you will
never find

Countless urges in your head
Sometimes, it feels, you are
better off dead

Feelings are hurt within every
opened door
once you think it's over, you go
out and seek more

Heart is locked to fight the
pain
so much, it's hard, figuring out
what's real or insane

You know it's a problem but
can't seem to change
Constant battle, in the mind,
it's like a gun range

With thoughts so loud, you
cannot sleep
you begin to listen, then start
to weap

Every feeling and experience is
locked in tight

you begin to wonder, why it is,
you fight

What is the point, when it
doesn't seem fair
why allow your heart to
experience the tear

Why keep that hope, for
something will change
why think positive, why feel so
strange

It's in your veins to feel
complete
mind and soul will finally meet

Your heart is broken, but still,
it's there
to show others, at least you
care

You have never been selfish, you
hide the pain
your heart is so big, even
through the strain

Often wondering how you have one
at all
you know that caring, is your
one true call

Inspirational in the eyes of
many, but to me,

I see no other way to be

*I don't need thanks, a smile
will do
my prize, is in, encouraging you*

*Encouraging others to see their
worth
has been named my calling since
my birth*

*I've been through hell but here
I stand
always willing, to lend that
helping hand*

*I experience torment within my
heart
vowing, to never, share a single
part*

*If you don't care, still know, I
do!
I'm here, for every, single one
of you*

Lurking In Darkness

*Laying awake on a thoughtless
night where the vision
of safety is disappearing from
sight*

*Red flags are waving, sharing a
belated goodbye
with darkness now falling on
trust that sufficed*

*Repetitive actions experienced
several times in life
with many intentions on
furthering the knife*

*One at a time they step to the
plate giving the belief
of "I'm different" then disaster
is fate*

*Trust isn't given to someone
each day, it's pretty much
banned because I like it that
way*

*Once given out you've earned a
place in my heart that will
still remain there after you've
torn it apart*

*I'm a soft-hearted girl with
pain in my eyes but I'm tough
as nails and see through lies*

*I won't be broken but you can
try, just know it's a waste
because I've faced many goodbyes*

*Be open, upfront, truthful and
clear don't hide in the
darkness and then just disappear*

MIND A RUNNING

I feel so tired
but yet I'm awake
My mind keeps running
but I need a break
A break from my thoughts
and visions so clear
Maybe go out on the town
and drink up some beer
Or stay home and erase all
thought
that people can be there
my disease can be caught
I shut off my heart
to keep out the pain
But yet it gets in
and gives my mind a strain
There is a fix
and that I can do
Just shut it out more
and continue on through
Through that door that remains
closed
can't be opened
no one is opposed
Build walls higher
than they remain now
And just say the hell with the
world
I've got the know how

Who are you?

Whisper softly, in my ear
Tell me the things, you want me
to hear

Tell me your truth, spare no
lies
Let me drift away, within your
eyes

Show me your heart and I'll
share mine
I want to know the things that
make you shine

I want to see your strengths,
admire your flaws
Accept the destiny, in which
your heart calls

What lifts you up? What brings
you down?
What makes you smile or causes a
frown

What made you the person you are
today
How do you tackle obstacles
standing in your way

What are the dreams, you hold
way up high

What passion exists that makes
you fly

Tell me what you've been
through, good and bad
What's the best experience you
feel you've had

Talk to me, tell no lies
I don't judge, I simply surprise

I listen, I learn, observe and
portray
What makes us the people we are
today

Curious minds, they want to know
The very things that make us go

Daily Struggles

We live to fight another day, some
will leave but some will stay

We fight to see that rising sun that
lets us know our search is done

We wish upon a shooting star that
faith is seen and not too far

A heart of gold thrown in the dirt,
we get back up and face the hurt

Petals are falling, surrounding the pain,
inside, the makings, of a breakless chain

So much hurt has been received, only image
that's plausible is being deceived

I hate the walls that I have built, trying to be
safe, leaving me full of guilt

Pushing away anyone who gets too close,

broken inside and it truly shows

I break my heart from day to
day, for I fear
that nobody will truly stay

I know that I am worth the wait,
but doubt
that love is in my fate

My walls are so high, no one
will wait
by the time its figured out, I'm
already too late

I'm distant and cautious, with
my heart,
for the fear of someone else,
tearing it apart

I'm strong as an ox, tough as
nails,
but I've experienced my guard
having it's fails

My heart is big, I cannot
change,
I still have hope even though
it's strange

I believe in good, still have my
doubt
sometimes it makes me want to
shout

I decide to fight, despite the pain
hoping one day, I will have gain

Divided in Thought

Heading down a path unknown
where success nor failure have
either been shown

Coming to a fork ahead, will you
take the one familiar
or get curious instead

One way you've been and decided
to settle while the
other you're afraid of and
always back pedal

Being safe is the way you know,
but taking risks
seems the way to go

True happiness lies in the path
unknown, and its one place,
you have never flown

You think about it in your head
and dream of it as you lay
down to bed

You want that feeling when you
wake, but with open eyes
it seems so fake

The only way you'll ever know
it's true, is to suck it up,

because it's up to you

COMING OUT

My mind isn't shallow
My mind is so bright
My heart sees through fear
on a cold winters night
My ego is big
but yet so true
You hurt me but
I won't hurt you
My vision is simple
valiant and brave
I'll stand through the hurt
and still won't cave
I'll walk through the fire
not run away
And in case you don't know
I am positively gay
Some don't agree
but I just don't care
Everyone deserves to be happy
and that's why I share
If it's a sin then check the
mirror
because all of your hatred
Is all so clear
Isn't it true that
You shall not judge
Or decide someone's life
gives you rights to a grudge
Everyone is equal
or so they say
But all of that changes
when you admit you're gay

I'd rather be gay
and hated by all
then to live a life of misery
and never truly fall
In love, for real
no lies, all true
I'd want that same happiness
for all of you

DON'T GIVE UP

The world is full

Of heartache and pain

A feeling well known

Yet hard to explain

Each one is different

But in some ways the same

There's never one reason

That always takes blame

Why so much emotion?

Why so much pain?

Why hearts are broken

Will never be explained

Move forward each time

Don't stay in the past

One day you will find

True feelings that last

No more tears will be shed

No more pain will be seen

You've just got to realize

That the world can be mean

Forgive and Forget

Forgive and forget

Is easy for some

But with a past like mine

It's easy to succumb

I can't forget

The life I was dealt

Or forgive the people

Who didn't care how I felt

They let it happen

But now it's past?

To me it's still real

And won't let go real fast

I still have memories

Of every awful day

Like slow motion in my mind

And won't go away

You think it's easy

Well believe it or not

The memories for me

Won't be forgot

Inescapable Chaos

Search really deep and you will
find, the rampant
chaos that controls my mind

Most don't care or even want to
know but the
struggle is real and it'll never
let go

It's like you're in a movie,
watching your life as it goes,
and danger is lurking, where?,
no one knows

Your guard remains solid because
you won't let it in,
you feel anything good, has bad
hidden within

When you've been hurt so much,
its then you will see,
that trust starts lacking and
caution breaks free

You are cautious without trying,
fear the unknown, hide
deep inside yourself, end up
feeling all alone

You carry on day to day,
determined that nothing

shall stand in your way

Your guard remains up, trust
almost banned, you fear
the touch of a helping hand

It's out of control, you know
it's true, but still you want
to run because that's all it
feels you can do

You don't want any more hurt so
you guard your heart, so
much to an extent where it can't
be torn apart

It seems sort of great because
it's safe to you but you can't
help
to wonder about opportunities
you have already passed through

Good may have passed by and you
wouldn't know, because
the chains on your heart refuse
to let go

So you move on and think hard
through the days, wondering if
ever you will change your ways

It seems unlikely because it's
been your way for years, but one

day, unexpectedly, you might
chase those fears

Everyday Battles

As I lay me down to sleep a
sudden
bad feeling has started to creep

I notice how my guard is down
and fear
hurt is coming so I start to
frown

This isn't the first time or the
last
but this hurt coming is unlike
the past

This time it's strange because
it seems so real
and heartbreak is coming, that's
how I feel

I linger in a thought so blind,
I'm numb to
the world, just trapped in my
mind

I'm lost in a silence, gazing in
space, a ghostly
look upon my face

Thoughts are flying, I'm dazed
and confused, I try

to find the answer but it has
been refused

I'm stuck in a dream as I try to
wake, hoping
to see that it's all been fake

I can't wake up, I've been stuck
for days, I'm
trapped in a nightmare, lost in
a maze

Searching for an exit, it should
be near, and
on the other side I'll fight
this fear

When I'm feeling down and my
mind is distraught
I think of past battles I've
already fought

It gives me the courage I need
to pull through
and gaining hope is what I do

I hope the insecurities in my
heart will one day,
soon, forever part

For now they stay, but my
courage is stronger
and fear will take over and win
no longer

I strive on being strong,
protection is key, if
I can save other people, I can
surely save me

Just One of Those Days

Nothing's going right

Just one of those days

Silence is bestowed upon

But sound decides to stay

Patience is a virtue

Frustration takes the scene

When you want a little peace

Everyone thinks you are mean

Anger starts a brewing

Deep inside you scream

Your only hope for happiness

Is to pretend it's just a dream

Close your eyes a few seconds

Maybe count to three

Go into a happy place

Remember what you see

Calmness starts occurring

Suddenly, you feel relief

You made it through a tough time

And caused no grief

Just a Little Insight

*What better to do on a rainy day
write a poem and fade away*

*Thoughts can flourish, peace
obtained
mental draining has been
sustained*

*Listen to the sound of the
falling rain
as it hits the ground, stimulate
my brain*

*Satellite not working, internet
is crap
enslaved in my mind, could be a
trap*

*My mind is entertaining all on
its own
strength and weakness both are
shown*

*My mind is a temple, my heart a
key
every instance that is yearning
for the best of me*

*Find the key to my mind and
you'll reach my soul
it's a treacherous journey,
where fear takes role*

My past is a burden, my future is bright
I've been through hell, still choose to fight

I'm learning to accept it, slowly letting go
in my heart, I can feel it show

Believing in things I didn't know I could
have to admit, it really feels good

I'm growing stronger, will soon be free
just a little insight, into the truth that's me

WISDOM OF THE HEART

The world is broken

Its falling apart

I feel this nonsense

Deep within my heart

Everyone wants love

To be loved so true

But look at all the heartache

It has put you through

Weakness makes us strong

But some remain weak

They got it figured out

And refuse to speak

They choose to be alone

Until it hurts so bad

They wish they had the love

From the ones they once had

When they find out they're gone

They then want them back

But the world has a way

Of derailing that track

If you are writing off loved ones

For wanting the best for you

Think really hard about

What you want to do

Words are wisdom
Hearts are true

Love is uncanny

You shouldn't feel blue

Love From Above

Valentines Day is a day of love

For those all around us

And the ones up above

Never forgotten

Remembered each day

Though no longer seen

In our hearts they stay

If I had one wish

I know what it'd be

That my loved ones in heaven

Could come visit me

It might sound crazy

I mean it's just one day

But I'd love the opportunity

To just say "hey"

Let them know that they are loved

And remain deep in my heart

And the day they left

Ripped my world apart

I'm still moving forward

Doing the best I can

I hope they are happy

And remain their #1 fan

Since I know that can't happen

I just wanted to say

To my loved ones in heaven

Happy Valentines Day

Birthday in Heaven

My dearest baby boy

You are up in heaven

Where today is the day

You are turning seven

It seems like yesterday

Though I know it's been years

Since I was able to hold you

And wipe away your tears

I miss you so much

And love you so true

You will always and forever

Be my baby blue

I hope you're still smiling

From ear to ear

Like you always did

Each day you were here

The room lit up

With one smile from you

Sadness was gone

And anger too

You are in my heart

Where you will always stay

I love you my son

Happy birthday

Judgement

*What do you see, when you look
in my eyes
Do you see the strength or only
cries?*

*How does it feel, staring into
my soul?
Do you see how fear has played
its role?*

*Have you noticed the heartbeat
within my chest?
Do you realize my intentions are
only the best?*

*Can you feel the warmth within
my heart?
Growing stronger each day, from
the very start*

*Do you recognize the kindness I
have for all?
Though, all around me, I've
built a wall*

*Did you notice I'm terrified of
getting too close?
For one day, hatred, always
seems it shows*

*I'm scared down deep but hide it
well
I still have hope, can't you
tell*

*I have a heart that leads me
blind
Fight a constant battle, between
heart and mind*

*Do you see I fight despite the
pain?
Rationally, I feel, it's sort of
insane*

*I found my heart, though, it was
lost
I will follow it now, despite
the cost*

*I fell in love, within a dream
Realize, to work, it takes a
team*

*Heart and mind must work as one
Never giving up, won't risk the
fun*

*I will continue to wait forever
on end
For fear, is a word, I can
comprehend*

Done

I'm done with the lies
done drying my eyes

Done believing in good
when it's only a disguise

Breaking up with my heart
We have had our fun

Tired of it breaking
so I'm completely done

I'm going to be heartless
never feeling again

Take a bow life
as you finally win

Screw everything, besides my
boys
They are the only thing left to
bring me joys

My boys are my heart, never
going to change
hope in others, I no longer
exchange

I'm done with the world, rid my
heart

Only hatred is coming to play
its part

Why be kind when all else is
mean
believing it could change was
definitely obscene

I toss my heart in to the sea
and that is the end of the good
in me

TIME FOR GOODBYE

As I lay awake
This warm summer night
My mind is wandering
My heart is in fright
As one part is open
Another will close
I can't be broken
That part has been froze
But yet people try
Each day of my life
They try to break me
And stab with a knife
I still keep trying
To gain trust with that one
Who will make it all better
Instead of break it for fun
But each time I try
It doesn't work as planned
It's the same thing all over
So trust is now banned
I'm tired of people
Who love to pretend
That they care about me
And are a real friend
When deep down inside
They know it's a lie
So now I think
It's time for goodbye

Wreckless in Fear

*A wounded soul clearly hidden
from sight
a guarded heart shown in an
abundance of light*

*A clever mind uncertain of trust
determined in any sense that it
will be a bust*

*Issues with trust I can't
explain
Irrational thoughts are what
keeps me sane*

*Chasing a dream to relinquish
the fear
though many times it has been
shown so clear*

*Determined to change it with
love in my heart
though my heart is broken and
falling apart*

*I search for a reason to change
my ways
Always ends in failure, and
then, fear stays*

*Walls grow higher surrounding a
beating heart*

*that has been broken and
bruised, each time taking a
small part*

*My heart no longer whole, my
mind no longer clear
leaving behind a life, fully
surrounded by fear*

*A tough exterior left by facing
it all
with chains so deep there is no
way to fall*

*When your heart has been broken
as much as mine
You can see how pain and fear
combine*

*It's almost at a point where I
cannot trust
But fighting that fear has
become a must*

*Trust may be minimized,
observance a key
but bravery and strength grow
strongly in me*

*I'm afraid to be hurt but know
I'll get through
This would be a testament from
me to you*

FREEDOM

I'm free as a bird

Flying way up high

Looking down on the world

And waving goodbye

Soaring through clouds

And places unknown

Remembering the places

I've already flown

The past is forgotten

The future will be told

I'll find out my meaning

As I start turning old

I'll look back on the bad times

But strive on the good

I'll stop being mad

About being misunderstood

All will be forgiven

My story done told

And I'll move through the wreckage

And stop feeling so cold

As I'm up here flying

And feeling so free

I will finally realize

This was all meant to be

Love

Soft touch
Great Skin
One heart
Will win
Your lips
So sweet
My heart
Will beat
You're here
I'm free
Our love
Will be
Everlasting
True
No longer
Feel blue
Our Souls
Connect
Together
Accept
Our love
So true
No one else
Will do
It's you
It's me
This love
Will be
One day
Real soon
Whistling
A tune

It's you
And me
Our love
Grows free

Much Thanks

I know, I have
a fragile heart

I've seen, I felt
it torn apart

I bleed, I've bled
I feel the pain

It's typical, uncanny
and radically insane

I trust less, deny more
love just the same

And no one, not anyone
could put out that flame

Then one day, out of nowhere
someone had changed

My mind, my thoughts
I felt so estranged

In a good way, not bad
just different for me

I'm growing, just a little
and feeling more free

I thank you, much thanks
that you understand

And took it, upon yourself
to lend me your hand

You're crazy, you're sweet
your hearts made of gold

And anyone, would be lucky
To have it to hold

Bleeding Heart

The heart wants what the heart
wants
In search of love, it hunts, it
hunts

Fear and terror play their part,
following the path of a bleeding
heart

Wanting love, but too afraid,
a fragile heart is easily played

Refusing heartbreak, no matter the
cost,
leaving the mind confused and lost

Anytime love gets too close,
distance comes in, leaving fear
exposed

Too few are willing to climb the
wall
breaking the barriers and gaining
it all

This love is magic, true, sublime!
All it takes is a little more time

If you have the patience and the
strength to shift,
this love could be a remarkable
gift

One of a kind, swear its true,
possibilities are endless and
given to few

Heart had a few nibbles and one
huge bite,
this time choosing its willing to
fight

Crazy as it seems, can't change
the mind,
leaving body and soul leading me
blind

I'm cautious without trying, fear
the unknown,
but over the years I can see I've
grown

This time is different, I'm seeing
a light,
my insides are stirring as my
heart took flight

My mind always wins, but this time
my heart,
It's taking over each and every
part

I will fight to the end, whether
days or years,
setting aside all my lifelong
fears

This is the feeling I hoped would
come, one day,
my mind finally took a break,
heart now in charge
and leading the way

Forbidden Love

Nothing comes close to forbidden love

Your heart is entangled and feelings won't shove

You're up all night, dreaming through the day

Wondering if only there was a way

You want to win the heart of the one you adore

You know you can't have it but want it much more

The harder you fight the feelings the stronger they get

You try to stop it, but love won't forget

Before you know it they're always on your mind

That one special person makes your heart so blind

You hold it in because you're tough

But after awhile it gets kind of rough

You want to scream it out for all to hear

But losing them becomes a fear

You see your life with them alone

And fear your heart will soon be shown

You bite your tongue in person but inside your head

You feel the butterflies and love them instead

It's not something that just goes away

Because inside, the feelings will always stay

Rumor has it

*I've heard this rumor going
around
that love is out and hit the
ground*

*Is it true? Could this be right?
In the instance, I choose to
fight*

*People say dating is out the
door
Sex is in and nothing more*

*I can't believe the words I hear
All because now, everybody has
fear*

*They're giving up, and I'm too
late
How do you get to know someone
without a date?*

*I've chosen to stay single,
because I want it all
Now that I've found it, only I
can fall?*

*It doesn't make sense, say it's
a lie
My heart has been opened, I
don't want to say goodbye*

The power I feel is hard to
believe
I've been struck by lightning,
still won't leave

Hypnotized by an image in my
mind
feelings within have been
outlined

Acting crazy, possibly going
insane
Either way it goes, I only see
the gain

Feeling things I've never felt
before
Love my reaction! Couldn't ask
for more!!

I'm overly excited, I'm ready to
start
Following the path, that leads
my heart

If I'm the only one, it's okay,
I'll survive!
But, I won't give up this
feeling, of being so alive

A Part of Me

It appears to be, I'm all alone
crying inside, while only strength
is shown

There has been a hole, placed in
my heart
that is repeatedly filled, then
emptied, piece to part

Never full, for it's too much to
bear
At this point, I'm too tired to
care

Not complaining, just stating a
truth
talking it out, in hopes, that it
goes away smooth

I've journeyed through hell,
staying the path
quit fighting the obvious, taken
the wrath

I hope for the best, get the worst
accept the outcome, my heart is
cursed

I expect the bad, get a glimpse of
good
I own the experience, as though I
should

I'm damaged, I know, but I am kind
I'm a good hearted soul, as anyone
that meets me can find

I hold on to the torture, that
surrounds my past
for pain in my life, is all that
seems to last

I'm great at goodbyes, because I
can't make you stay
I try to enjoy the time I get,
until you walk away

The story of my life, its written
in blue
take it as it comes, there is
nothing else to do

I can handle pain, my biggest
strength
I take it so kind, my compassion,
no length

I do have issues, especially with
trust
It's the one thing, I've seen,
that's an oblivious bust

I have PTSD, it comes, it goes
only fear is, the thought, of when
it shows

People see me as strong, the world
is my own

I never intend to, let weakness be
shown

Weakness is feeling, I can
comprehend
because when I feel, the world,
appears to end

I do feel, though I try to not
doesn't work that way, I have been
caught

I feel so deep, down to my soul
but hiding the feelings, has been
named, my goal

I hide them well, but sometimes
they slip
take a walk with me, it's worth
the trip

My mind is intelligent, my heart
is kind
my compassion is beauty, sometimes
leading me blind

I have a lot to say, and I will
make it clear
I am not scared, I have no fear

My past is only a shadow, not what
is meant to be
It's a crazy, hard truth, that's
also, a part of me

I Care

I see this world inside my mind
Obstacles are everywhere! But,
the end, I'll find!

While some see the world as
beautiful and bright
I also see the darkness and to
fix it, I fight!

My strength is wicked, my mind,
extreme!
My hopes are so high, I dream
and dream

I won't fall in, to the depths
of hell
I've experienced the torture,
and the pain, I know well

You may think I'm weak, but, I
assure you, I'm strong
Anyone that knows me, will say
you're wrong

If you knew the pain, I hide in
my heart
You would change your outlook
from the very start

If you knew the hell that I
survived

*You would wonder, how, my heart
arrived*

*Even I don't know, it's
questioned each day
I have no idea, how I turned out
this way*

*My heart is big, my
intelligience, strong
They have been that way, all
along*

*I know pain so well, I would
never share
instead, I choose, to always
care*

*I'll care when you're hurtful,
I'll care when you're mean
I'll care like nothing you have
ever seen*

*I will always be good, never
turn bad
Even when pain, is all I've had*

*I will care until my end, my
heart shines bright
on my darkest days, you will
still see my light*

*Heart on my sleeve, fire in my
soul*

kindness for all, is a number
one goal

Water me down, sprinkled in dust
I live in peace, with a heart, I
must

Love as a Fairytale

Come with me, my love, take my hand
Together, we shall drift to a fairytale land

You, be my queen, and I the rock
That keeps us together, despite all the talk

We'll sail through seas, and storm the skies
My journey begins, staring deep in your eyes

We'll travel through mountains, and forests, alive!
Any danger that is lurking, we most definitely survive

We'll conquer the world, with you by my side
There is no time for running or trying to hide

I see me slaying dragons to rescue my queen
Holding her tightly, when life gets mean

Despised by many, acknowledged by few

Only opinion that matters, is
the one from you

I've battled the demons
surrounding my past
Now, I'm ready, for a true love
that lasts

Whether good times or bad, I
know we'll make it through
Then one day a question, the
answer? I do!

Our journey continues, growing
stronger each day
The love in our eyes never going
away

Join me, my love, let us take a
stand
Destiny is waiting, in the palm
of your hand

Stay

I don't want, to lose you again

*Battle of my life, has started,
I'm determined to win*

I don't want, to see you go

*Once was enough, twice would
blow*

I don't want, you to walk away

Come to me, please, just stay

*The pieces that are left, of my
broken heart*

I give to you, every single part

*Please don't run, stay, lets
chill*

*The rush, you give me, I'm
deemed to feel*

*I can't say "I love you" but
feel I might*

*Every ounce of my being says
"stay" and "fight"*

Come back to me, don't leave so soon

I am the sky, and you, the moon

I kneel to you, amongst trying times

With heartfelt words, and intense rhymes

I vow to you, I will numb the pain

As peaceful, the sound, of falling rain

As beautiful, the vision, of the stars

As swift, the speed, of passing cars

I will never let go, my feelings are true

My whole heart, I give to you

It's Okay

*It's okay to let me go
I realize now, it was for the
show*

*Caught up in the excitement, I
lost my way
Thinking, whole-heartedly, you
could be mine one day*

*The feelings I get whenever you
are near
Leave my mind blown and thinking
unclear*

*I'm not another pervert, sitting
down at the bar
Playing out a fantasy, while
staring from afar*

*I don't go to the club to see
girls strip
The conversation, to me, is
worth the trip*

*I believe you've built a world,
inside your head
Feel you can't escape, so you
live it instead*

*I don't think you realize the
feelings you've hurt*

But, I thank you for unlocking,
the chain on my shirt

I've never been one to believe
in love
But, you gave me hope that arose
from above

I'm still not mad, if anything
relieved!
At least one time, I truly
believed

I wish you well and hope one day
you find
The world I live in, which to
you, seems blind

The world is scary, it's a
terrible place
But, you are missing the good,
written all over your face

Have a little faith and try to
believe
Happiness is out there, though
hard to achieve

Have an open heart let nothing
stand in the way
True happiness will be yours,
eventually, one day

Finding My Feelings

I know what love is, and I know
what it's not
I've battled through both,
battles well fought

I will always be the bigger man
I will always be honest, because
"I can"

I would never lead one on, to
play a game
messing with emotions is
definitely lame

If you can't be upfront, don't
say a word
Lying is out, or haven't you
heard

I've guarded my heart, to let no
one in
but, you pushed on through so, I
guess you win

I've accepted the reality, yet,
still I cry
In the very instance, of
knowing, I must tell you goodbye

It hurts so bad, destroyed, is
my heart

but, I'll put it back together,
part by part

My heart, it yearns, for the
warmth of you
but, that warmth is turning
cold, with nothing I can do

I lay awake, each and every
night
searching, for the smallest
option, to make me fight

The reasons are lessening, I'm
growing scared
for you are the first, with
whom, my heart, I shared

I never knew love, until I met
you
but, now it seems, love, makes
me blue

What if now, I won't try again?
for love, it hurts, so, my
guard, will win

I feel me giving up, if I let go
My heart is yours, just letting
you know

My heart is open, my dreams
collide

*Something is stirring, deep
inside*

*The storm is brewing, I'm ready
to fight
I'm following the path, I feel
is right*

*The path of my heart, it leads
to you
I know, inside, the feelings are
true*

*On the outside, it appears, this
battle is lost
On the inside, however, fingers
are crossed*

*I hope I'm not crazy, I hope
it's real
because I finally learned, what
it is, to feel*

CPSIA information can be obtained
at www.ICGtesting.com
Printed in the USA
LVHW080954311018
595461LV00010B/59/P